Swans

Swans

poems

Michelle Brown

Palimpsest Press
1171 Eastlawn Ave.
Windsor, Ontario. N8S 3J1
www.palimpsestpress.ca

Printed and bound in Canada
Cover design and book typography by Ellie Hastings
Edited by Jim Johnstone

Palimpsest Press would like to thank the Canada Council for
the Arts and the Ontario Arts Council for their support of our
publishing program. We also acknowledge the assistance of the
Government of Ontario through the Ontario Book Publishing
Tax Credit.

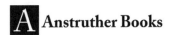

LIBRARY AND ARCHIVES CANADA CATALOGUING IN PUBLICATION

TITLE: Swans : poems / Michelle Brown.
NAMES: Brown, Michelle, 1989- author.
IDENTIFIERS: Canadiana (print) 20230147151
             Canadiana (ebook) 2023014716X

ISBN 9781990293436 (SOFTCOVER)
ISBN 9781990293443 (EPUB)
CLASSIFICATION: LCC PS8603.R6923 S93 2023 | DDC C811/.6—DC23

For J & K, forever my main characters

And for Zoë, forever

Contents

Unwearied still, lover by lover,
They paddle in the cold
Companionable streams or climb the air;
Their hearts have not grown old;

— "The Wild Swans at Coole," William Butler Yeats

'Swans Watering Hole' Dance Floor,
after *Wild Swans*

You, who watch from the shore,

dip your toes in and think you invented flight.

I'm not entirely sure you know what a swan is.

Nineteen autumns and you think we're still waiting for you?

Tread lightly: we covered the water with glass.

We're not peace. We're not your private dancers.

Feathers featureless. Muscles ready to jaguar.

The bell-beat of wings is a warning

as you ignore our violence, bend our necks into hearts.

Getting There

Ada holds out her hands saying *pick one*.

I'm driving and we're late so I just reach over.

I touch something round like a pearl.

I think it's gum but who knows.

Who knows if what I chose was the correct answer.

Or if the game was to not choose at all.

If it was only to get my attention.

To hit gravel and look at her:

look, this could be a *moment*,

the two of us laughing in the dark,

the proportions of our bodies still equidistant,

still swapping jean shorts, still letting her cut my bangs.

A self-sufficient economy. A universe you forget

you're floating in until you see a mirror.

To pull over the stupid car, climb out and over the fence,

run back the other way, protecting each other from a lifetime

of different lanes; choosing her.

A Line That Snakes All the Way Around to the Future

From back here, the future looks like two doors guarded by one man. The weather is nothing. There arc no job prospects. I hold your hand or bite it and get fed either way. My bad behaviour is still cute and I string it behind *bubbly* on my list of marketable adjectives. The future is getting closer and looks like it's going to be busy. The gatekeeper isn't impressed by my whimsy or my sequins. And those are my only two tricks. My body still listens to me. My hair springs into curls like raised hackles as I heckle him. No go. The future's full, already breaking fire codes. I try everything I can to pass the time. I kick at the heels of the people in front of me. I trim my split ends with pocket scissors and spread the leftovers like seeds in the wind. Pick glitter out of my teeth. We shuffle forward and now I'm trapped in front of a dark window, staring at my own face superimposed over the future people. Shi and Ada and Bri and Guy are already inside. Allison is dropping off drinks. It's my birthday party. Their heads are bent together in a beautiful circle; an anklet that keeps me chained to them, buzzing if I move further away. Vincent shows up, shoves a paper bag in my hand and leaves. The line was too long and he didn't want to wait. Inside is a tall can of beer and a Bruce Springsteen album. Maybe he'll come back later, when I'm a little closer.

Spells for Drunk Girls

Make it a double. Define *trouble*.
A cinnamon heart. Empty deodorant stick.
Secondhand eyeshadow palette.
Table for 18, separate bills.

A load-bearing brick.
Mourning in public.
Count 'em all: 10 fingers, 10 toes.
A single kiss on the tip of my nose.

Misremembered birth time.
A slip on a silk scarf.
Incense burn.
Define *assault*.

Charcoal filtered through my stomach.
I was found behind the booth.
A backpack on an empty bus.
Penicillin bracelet. Last baby tooth.

A tree to climb in the distance.
Cut hairs stuck to your cheek.
Another way to hurt my mom.
COOLPIX 300 with a flipped screen.

New tattoo: *come and get me.*
Text to dad: 'come and get me.'
A fistful of wet hair.
Define how he touched me.

A roommate who stayed.
Cute drool.
Single scissor blade.
Define *champagne.*

Same Three Friends in Different Universes

In this one, we're deer leaping into electric fences.

In another, we're three drunk girls sleeping it off under the table.
That sticks for a while.

In this one, we go only by our first names;
I try to find them in the phone book,
give up after I.

In this one, the prettiest time-travels back
and we sit wrinkled in the gallery at her debut,
far beneath a line of backup dancers.

In another, we're three marbles in a match against each other
without knowing where the floor will end
or who set us off on this hellish death race.

In this one, we never meet at all and are honestly fine.
Who has time to lose each other?

In another, we were pretty good friends until we graduated
and because we hadn't played *never have I ever* enough,
keep our weekly phone calls to a tidy twenty, scrubbed of secrets.

In another, one of us die and the other two write books about it:
a mediterranean cookbook, and a diary burned and thrown off a cliff.

In this one, one deer escapes.

In this one, the correct one, we pile into a backseat,
heads in laps, teeth out, our driver desperate to rearrange us.

Us three who have never been hurt yet hurt handily,
each second chance we're given.

The Dancer

Her hands in prayer
then jubilantly thrown

cast devils at bystanders.
She steps boxes around them,

circles the room, checks for traps
in the floor with pointed toes.

Taps twice and the ground opens.
Swallowed, I'm here trying not

to embarrass my young self,
undone by even my own hair,

my own shadow's curve.
When they told me to pray,

this is what I was promised:
a girl like me who likes me.

The Witness

Shining! Shimmering! Splendid!
I shout. We're at the docks.

Imagine ending a world tour
with a polite sign off.

Not in your vocabulary.
Your soft, spiked hair a halo.

It's the only time you've told a lie.
From down here, Swans is just a story.

I'm afraid but you don't call me on it.
Loving you is being watched by you.

Every muscle mirrored.
Every ring on the trunk matched.

I'll take you anywhere, I start.
You can't sing, but you agree.

You never take me far.
But you ask me where I want to go

and I answer. Then
no but where do you really want to go.

The Historian

I was put here
to love them.
To put them down
in writing.
To write myself
as a person they might
love back.

Pitchers of Raspberries

You can hold her hand.

You can help yourself.

You can fall asleep under the table,

a silver-dipped palm stroking your hair.

You can get up and grow.

Ignore the bartender who claims

you're bad for business, ignore the memory

until years later when you shoulder her on the sidewalk,

home again for the holiday upheaval.

You can hold her

and not understand

until years later what it was,

that hot pit in your stomach

that twisted like a girl's tongue,

pulling and pulling out into a knot,

tighter all this time,

to finally untie it.

It's fine to not know.

It's fine to want more

and still feel wasted the next morning

by the sweet, high percentage.

Karaoke at 10 p.m.

Is your daddy home?
My power, my pleasure, my pain —
Did he go and leave you all alone?
There's so much a man can say.

My power and pain!
For a smile, we share the night.
There's so much a man can say —
pay anything to roll the dice.

For a smile, we share the night.
Little high, little low.
Anything to roll the dice.
Will you let me go?

Little high, little low.
Did he leave you all alone?
Now that your rose is in bloom.
Will you let me go?

The Dancer Requests

If they won't play your song
it was never yours at all —
melody snagged in a net
and made to dance in some dank
basement studio; while you
imagine yourself to be the addressed,
he couldn't sing the dark syrup
of your sadness, could only hope
to syncopate snaps over it. To shrink
to his bars you'd need to straighten
your woozy waltz, dampen your deep drum,
and if he were really to run you up
on a dance floor east of midnight,
he'd rescind his rights to it all,
bow to your shuffle, strum
only your taut backbone,
wish he'd never written down
the notes you pocket as you descend
the scale, writing your own.

Ugly Duckling

A duckling is as similar to a swan
as two ducklings are to each other,

said Aristotle, who'd never had
to dance beside a prettier friend.

If he had, to reciprocate good
will, would've scratched his own face

to bring her into the light,
thrown himself into the bevy

of feathered assholes,
suicidal for her sake.

Men love their friends
for their own good

and women love their
friends the way they want

to be loved: flung-open
door, bonded for life,

though divorce can occur
in nesting failure.

How much longer
can I hold your shoes

in the rain while you
bandage your feet?

Forever. Aristotle divorced
Athina after Maria Callas

sang to him in the shower.
Her highs were unimaginable,

her violence deeper, subsurface.
She reminds me of you,

as you often remind me.
I don't need to gaze into a puddle

to know that the form of things matter.
Dodged that crossbow.

Pointed feet you can't see.
Too easily gliding across

the lake of tears.
Aristotle would choke.

In his two kinds of motion,
violent or natural,

where would he place you
in your final form,

dying headfirst
into the water.

OK let's go around the table and each share one weird thing

I'm 19 but I look 20.

I can see the heft of your breast in that dress.

I once inserted a crystal into her.

I met Murakami and Stallone at the same party.

I walked into the ocean with a pocket full of rocks.

I was born a faun.

I just kissed her in the hallway.

I'm the bassist.

I'm the fire marshall and this close to arresting all of you.

I bought a round and no one thanked me.

I slide my finger underneath your bra strap.

I drive a pick up and no one knows where I go.

I hear everything you say about me.

I'm Michelle's mom?

I'm returning to my planet.

I just met you but you guys seem fun.

I put my whole fist in her mouth.

I have so much power, they won't believe you.

I believed in god until she flicked her tongue.

I'm the third person.

I threw out my snow globes.

I moved here a week ago.

I'm a piece of beach glass, who are you?

I'd like to borrow that extra chair?

I saw you here yesterday.

I'm your red heart and I heard it all.

I just need to settle up.

I pierced my own tongue.

I was almost olympian.

I dream of owning a high-yield investment.

I'm bald underneath.

I want to live inside your warm mouth.

I'm a pilot to the stars.

I watched my brother shower.

I just need to settle up.

I think I'll stay.

You guys seem fun.

I think you guys seem fun for now.

Passed Around

He slid a finger under my bra like he was opening a letter.

Better, he marks my breast out loud.

Proud, like proving displacement theory.

Clearly we're both fucked. Maybe for the rest of time.

Chimes. The wind blows away what we were passing around,

found years later. Made into a bookmark or a book.

Look: I didn't know it was wrong that night.

Righting his words, rhyming his rhymes.

The Magician

He appears out of nowhere rarely ends well.
It could be years until you notice

how he altered your life like a hook
around your waist, pulling you off the dance floor.

He appeared out of nowhere. He sat down,
laid one palm open on the table and hid the other.

I read it as he started up my leg:
a long life, a happy happy happy life.

I don't believe it, I say.
But it happens in front of my eyes.

The whole thing: children / dogs,
cut vegetables clogging the sink,

cancer and his hand around my jaw,
a pressure that shakes something good out of me.

He appeared like a hand starting the magic show:
gloved, so you can't see the trick, so you just go for it.

Where'd she go, the crowd asks.
She's right here, she's in the wings,

waiting for another song
or a better magician.

The Incident

I don't remember it so I don't feel bad about it.

I don't feel bad about it until I see a rip in a nylon tent.

I don't remember anything but I have an aversion to nosebleeds.

It hasn't affected me in any way whatsoever, then the examining doctor says *relax, like a vice grip down there*!

I rank 1 out of 10 on the 'do you ever get sad' questionnaire and it also turns out the Disney Princess I'm most alike is Snow White, as previously suspected.

As previously suspected, he continued in his role as the president of the Student Peace Coalition.

Maybe he's right: it is nice that a beautiful woman woke up in his bed.

That beautiful woman being me. I don't feel bad about being beautiful.

But now I trace my steps. Leave crumb trails up to every bedroom. Trip wires across doors.

I don't remember much. *Will you publish this poem*, the professor cared.

If only to start putting things down. Start leaving them there.

Older MFA Student

Catch yourself in the mirror
and there I'll appear:
a moth banging on your lamp,
a lozenge stuck on your molar.

+

It's a secret I'll keep forever,
unlike the others I give up daily:
palm scars, black cheeks,
smoking in order to die.

+

Are you aware of the position
you're putting me in? he asked.
My position: play dead
instead of fight to the death.

+

Within your body
you can always find
a deeper bunker,
a more dangerous mine.

+

I tried to signal the others
through the walls.
This place is haunted.
Leave half of the rent.

+

Stop trying to write him
into every apology letter,
notice of termination,
missing cat poster.

+

I drink too much.
I am in a calm sea,
inches beneath
the turbulent *me.*

+

Consider my position:
not as prestigious as yours
but higher above,
heavy, an anvil.

Poet Voice

The buds in May drift towards the drain.
The buds they may. In solitude I drift away.

Where are my critics? Where are their words?
The sky is dark as a dark-winged bird.

Darker than scat. What's the word
for the thought before that?

O. It's O. Round mouthed thing.
And I am nothing. A cellphone rings.

I was alone in a room masturbating at the wall.
Throwing my voice, my head AWOL.

The garage backboard clanged. My brain came loose.
When I move to Japan my son will come too.

He'll bring his hoop and his best attitude.
I hate this poem. I hate all of you.

I hate that your faces are lit up in blue.
Repent, yells the most damaged man in the room.

Hello? I'm trying to describe solitude?
Where are the gasps? I'll gasp for you.

I'll wrench. I'll resume.
I told my wife I'd be home by two.

So what will I do if you're all leaving now?
The frothy glasses are crowding my gaze.

I'm afraid I can't keep up with your pace.
My son texted me an upside-down face.

What's wrong? What changed?
When will the fog resume its refrain?

Pet Name

He kisses her, a surprise.

Calls her his otter.

Until a better future,

I hold a rock

and float beside her.

Passerby

Enroute to Alaska on the *Allure of the Sea,*
we docked in the harbour

to buy wool socks and chocolate hedgehogs.
My wife returned to the ship while I carried the bags.

I carried them along the water until I hit a wall.
I saw three girls trying to climb it with a running start.

Their hair tied in a palomar knot
that hours couldn't untangle,

fingers fish-hooked to each other.
I wanted to walk into the sea.

Instead, I watched them give up
and crawl the grassy hill instead.

I called our daughter across the water,
static cresting her delicate soprano.

How's the trip, she asked without interest.
I looked around the parking lot.

I could hear the girls screaming.
With joy, I thought.

I rolled up my trousers.
On my hands and knees.

*You don't get many new beginnings
in this unending life,* I replied.

I'm over the hill now.
I come bearing gifts.

Wait, er

Overserved, the three of them
scare away good tippers with a snarl.

Who's to say says the one
waking up from a nap.

She was under the table
until we seated her,

my tray of raspberry sours missing,
their lips a guilty red.

*Who's to say if
we already paid!!!*

Cold to their charms,
I study on my phone.

Cleopatra was a drunk
but at least she'd luxuriate in it.

There's no gristle to this.
Nothing to chew and spit.

Transfixed, despite myself,
I watch as they smoke one cigarette,

laughing, adulated,
close enough to kiss.

I'm old enough to know
how these things go:

they think the centre of the universe contracts
them to stay linked forever

when really it expands, blackening,
until it's a phone call, a text, then nothing.

Fruit Fly

I'd do it all again.

Drown myself in sweet vinegar for a taste.

To have had you once is enough.

Who knows if I'll return.

Who knows if I'll return as a ghost

or a butterfly.

Two Dogs Bark in Neighbouring Garages

I'm at the sink and you're by the dryer.

Your mind is an unpickable flower.

Will we grow peaceful alongside each other?

Or be old and still throwing our weight at the door?

Scaring the kids who take a wrong turn.

Your breath fogs against the living mirror.

Bangs and hems trimmed with the same scissors.

Lockets of hair forgotten under your sweater.

If we met in the alley, out of our cages.

Wild. Without mothers.

How close would we be?

How close we were.

To killing each other.

Woman Rowing a Boat Emoji

Keep going.

1 in 3

Just barely above water,
the three of us dangle our toes in.

We left the bar as missing people,
heard our names being called,

then shouted, then forgotten.
We give ourselves new ones:

1, 2 and 3.
1 has been #1 for a while now,

adding gold medals
to her everyday stack.

2 and 3 don't mind.
They know 1st is worst.

And she honestly kind of is,
chilling her calves

until her legs wear a pink line,
feeding cigarettes to the fish.

2 and 3 know if anything happens
to them, tumours or divorce,

it's 1 in 3. At least we'll know
by name who walks back first,

heels in hand,
to pay what she owes.

Mid

An observer parachutes in.
It's you, standing at the bookshelf,
thumbing to where the spine cracks in two.
Thought you'd cut straight to the tension.
I'm still in it, so I'll read along with you.
I know the characters, if only by name.
Who might look at the camera first.
Who's going through the soft middle of it.
There are certain expectations that we both share.
That you exist. That I provide you with something truthful.
And that you pretend to believe it.
The pearl at the beginning was placed on purpose.
I hope it'll come in handy, played at the right moment.
Hurled at my feet or passed between teeth.
If you make it to the end before I do,
tell my friends I mean no harm
by whatever follows.
If by pinning them down
I've kept us here a page longer;
before Betty calls Al, before
the lights flood us out, before
embers light up the grate
and the taxi drives away,
before they both disappear
into the retelling, before they're
a tale I tell the both of us, each thumbing
through a life, hoping to forecast
the thundering end.

The Big One

They've got plans for me,

check my fault lines daily.

Do I cause you worry?

What if I lie very still.

What if I am a perfect circle.

In five or fifty years, they say,

she might develop a tremor.

Or it could be the big one.

The pendulum swinging

out of my favour.

As kids, we'd brace

our bodies under desks

as the intercom rumbled.

I'm there still, overserved,

protecting my neck.

Just closer to morning

and further from home.

Those of us who

didn't wait out the aftershocks

died almost immediately.

Dirt erupting like a celebration.

I know it'll happen.

I just don't know when.

Under The Table

And here I thought

I was looking at the stars.

The only constellation:

name, number, knifed.

It's the first time I've known

how to get in touch with god.

Would I like to have a good time?

Is that even a question?

who taught you

whose sweat beads into pearls

like hers. who swears to never tell

the thoughts we rack up.

who taught you how to dance.

who taught you how to dance

like that. i have a throat's worth

of secrets to sword dance over.

fall on the blade and our arches collapse.

who dares watch us. who dares throw pennies in.

i test my feelings. why not swallow them.

i smuggled in a cunt's worth of worry.

it's my identity. i am the master

of my own thoughts. i resist the bait.

i put it all back. who taught you

how to dance like that. i wrote it in a note:

i don't know why i feel this way. i prayed.

i held her hand inside my future. i fell on the blade.

pressed through me like a gust of wind. i cleaved.

i caved. who sweats this way. she's bathed in light.

i might. i might. i might. i might.

BFF

I nearly made the relay team but had to watch
as you sailed the finish line, wrapping it around you.
I was fifth but first to you, even above your mother and pet.
When you took me to your beach house I thought I'd died.
I ran smaller footprints behind you, so far behind
that you'd disappear for years, a decade.
Ten, and you locked me up.
If no one else is concerned, I'm not concerned.
But who am I without you? Still raw from the shower
where you dug handfuls of sand from my hair. Sam loved you
but he could only write letters. I could cartwheel around it.
Dive in holding your hand, holding you down for a minute,
in this blue green cold shimmering shimmering season.

Cam Girls

I wanted to be your mirror so I got one too.
Perched above the monitor like a pet bird,
it chirped and you came into view:
five months and a lifetime ahead of me;
perfect posture, eyes and hair the green and black
of 0s and 1s. I loved to make you laugh.
I loved imprinting our faces onto the future.
My face window over your face window.
Our pagers only had two buttons
for all the words I wanted to say: *are u growing up
w/o me* took days. I'd wait while you were at soccer,
retrace where you'd applied my white eyeliner.
My parents worried around the edge of the frame.
Each morning we got dressed together: butterflies
pinned above each ear, red bandanas loose around
our necks, covering two broken hearts on chains.
Sometimes I'd hold the camera in my hands
and show you my view:
the girl of the millennium, so bright against
the beige of your room, your lesser siblings,
each tendon and blink a beauty
our bitrate couldn't match.
Once, I talked to your empty backpack
slung across your chair.
Someone other than you found me
inconsolable in the bathroom.
I never looked for you after you left,
though every so often I'd plug it back in,
wait for the green light.

pillow slip

do girls like
girls like me

girls like girls
and boys

who swallow
whole thoughts

like a sick bird
like a book of jokes

told at funerals
incensed at the altar

of my unwavering
indecision

turning to the cooler
side of the pillow

sleeping through
the sleepovers

do girls like me exist
i slipped the note

under her bedroom door
though she must have lost it

i'm living the question
i'm turning my cheek now

both sides
flushed and grinning

Question Period

There was no help
for girls like me:

thumbing through BUST,
summer of 7th grade,

for a yes/no question
that'd confirm it,

after scrubbing off the bathroom wall
she wants to scissssssor

because I'd lingered too long
on her Juicy Couture velour sweats,

my brain gone serpentine, searching
for wetness like a finger held to the wind.

Feeling something was cut
with the absence of feeling,

a cluster of shame
or a stomachache.

There was no manual
for *I just want to hold her hand in the dark,*

toboggan down her slicked black hair
with the back of my wrist,

no piece of art I could see myself in
when I saw myself looking too long,

caught cleaved in the gorge of my new body,
church bench grooves in my knees,

when what I wanted was gruesome,
for god to say *hey I've got this one!*

I wanted to weave friendship
bracelets without the tension

and watch a Julia Roberts movie
without being caught — *was I?* —

by her mouth, by my mouth miming
how she said *I want you* to the men.

To be both ways at once,
to at least ask the question.

Remember fairyland. Looks nice. Lots of wildflowers.
Love you.
— text from Dad, 8:52 pm EST.

Remember closed rooms? What about the black thought that stained the tablecloth at Thanksgiving? Remember the woods that wove their way through my dresser? All of the boots were stomped. All of the horrors and holly hung. Remember what you told me at my birth party? You said *yes* and then I was your daughter. Just really open to whatever was coming. And what ended for you then, passing over your life like a waterbug? Was there a dream I stole that I ride now, on the bus into another black hole night? Am I your thought or a pattern you birthed, that unfurls into a life you can't fathom? A body that contains parts of you as a cracked mirror might. That we are partners walking in each other's shoes. I think I could cry, dad. I think I could love you as much as the flowers you pulled. As much as the photo you sent, megapixels blurring and beating. And when I find my words I'll welcome them like my own child and text back *yup, so beautiful, miss you, how could i forget.*

Wild Swans

What leaves will you blow over me?

    It's so sorrowful to not know yourself

    from a photo of yourself.

To feel wanted you need

to have matter and/or float

when thrown.

What heart.

It's important to know

your matter: my bones

are set to float when challenged.

I run through the field.

I catch up to you.

I want to lie

with you lies

in my upper

stomach — the trap door

in the stage. It's another

season and you still haven't

reappeared.

I'm melting

around the edges.

Hot plum.

New calf.

Baby tooth.

See?

She tilts her head to stretch out a headache
as the tide drags back, flattening itself
if only to slide under her feet.
I don't want to tiptoe in or roll up my pant legs.
I want to win. I want to swim.

SHOUTED FROM ACROSS THE BAR

My body taut
like a sick tiger.

My body thinks we're on to something.
Killing flies in the bathtub.

Checking the backyard for traps.
We're just one zipline ride away

from the rest of our lives.
Are you still okay?

Can you remove this stain
with your spit and thumb?

I'm not trying to invoke you.
I should bring it back to the tiger.

The tiger at the beginning.
The one who was crawling for you.

Karaoke at 1:30 a.m.

Save for the dog barking around back,
the bartender pummelling waters,
the younger girls shimmering and spitting,
the chairs toppling, the tables dancing,
the man saying *shhh shut up* to his dog,
Big John rustling names out of his fishbowl,
save for the boy of twelve, maybe twenty,
singing Celine with a hand to his throat,
for the woman in the apartment above,
with one hand to the moon, drowning him out,
save that story for a more generous time,
saved just for this lean hour when I can slip my palm
against your belly as you take a breath to sing.

Through the Glass

In a last attempt at coherency,
I lifted my head:

It's okay to be
what you are not to be.

I believe I believed it then,
tipped enough to see myself

through a milk glass.
Pure, carved from ice.

Held up to the stout,
the world looked to be

a thick sludge of trauma
sloshing in a small, dark sea.

It's what it'd turn out to be.
But then, that night,

the band was playing for me.
They played both *Michelle* and *My Michelle*,

and I believed them both.
That I was good and gruesome.

Your belle who never can tell.
Who does her dope for free,

words that go together well.
I asked the band to play it again,

then got behind the keyboard
and gave myself an encore.

I played it well: no one would know
until years later when I'd get healthy

and reveal this bottom of the well stuff.
Let people stumble over it like a skywalk.

From a bird or a plane,
these thoughts look like patches

on a quilt. One worn
out from thumbing it.

I left the dance floor
through the window.

It's not as violent as it sounds.
Someone opened it for me.

They saw me dancing alone
to my own songs and thought:

let's get this part
over with.

The Longest Creature in the World!!!!!

Or might be, they stipulated.
No one, not even the scientists,

had a desire to dive deeper on this:
we've seen it and it's horrible.

150 feet of mouths kissing
other mouths to form a body.

It's been growing for decades,
a suggestion of time that implies

progeny, even grandchildren,
but it could be as young as twenty-four.

Undoubtedly the worst age.
I barely made it.

So I do feel a kinship.
I don't feel afraid

when I dip my toes into the ocean
and the ocean bites back.

When I have a sharp thought,
one that digs like a nail in a palm,

I imagine it connecting to all the thoughts
that came before it, mouth to mouth,

to form a version of me.
The longest me in the world.

The me who prayed
until they swept the pews,

the me who loved my best friend
enough that I tried to die for her,

the me who begged him, in spring
by the woodshed, to beg me,

the me who unfurled,
the me who talked around it

until the psychiatrist said *there's nothing
wrong with her she's just a liar,*

imagine if I could reach back and hold her,
as the scientist cries and says on TV

*you can see old perished colonies that are still
attached but no longer alive,*

though they are, they're a hand skimming
the water as we swim, they're geraniums,

it's like seeing an ancient forest,
and it seems simple-minded

but past me didn't know you could love two things
at once: soft and hard, jubilantly connected.

I throw a cigarette into the water
and watch it sink to the very bottom.

How proud you must be
to have grown to fool them.

A creature whose existence seems disastrous,
when you're really just an endless chain

of small and soft bodies,
clinging to each other.

Closing Time

The taxi drivers roll the windows down.
The teens warm the pepperoni.
The busker opens his case.
The moms sit up in bed.
The corner store plays classical.
The emergency room strategizes.
The stranger's bed beckons.
The moon shines unclouded.
The sea sirens.
The boundaries sweeten like sugar and dissolve.
The three of us become two, one.
The one who won't leave, the historian.

You stand up too quickly
and the lights come on
at once. Everything you feared
is now in front of you:
They're packing up the keyboard.
He protects her head as she ducks
the taxi door. The hallway kissers
have gone home to their husbands.
The moon says it's true that
you've never been beautiful,
and you fall over.

wind me like a clock

stiff limbs pointing to your

birth time

I read your body

like a chart

the freckle in your iris

is autumn rising

the freckle on your shoulder

suggests I have to touch you

to know you

every   day we drink

every day we get better

we feel so good we kiss

the floor   the ceiling

is the underside of the table

we can touch the sky i've tried

i'm   sick   i'm   shy

i watch them kiss in the hallway

i've felt   the same

since i was   ten   we pray

then chassé   box step

on   graves

are u ok   ????

i tell time   who's boss

if it's me   you're looking for

i'll be   out by 1

or 2   or 3

i'll be the one driving

the   taxi

the band is packing up

one high hat rolls down

the stairs at me and i'm up

i'm awake i'm me i'm ready

i want to love you unduly

i'm ready for silence

with the odd cymbal

It's already tomorrow.

Who said we weren't

ready for the future?

Answers to a Few Private Questions

You're not too old
to paint a wall

to bite a finger
at the dentist

to call him back
with a changed name

to glue on
a bigger eyelash

to take a sip
and return it

to change your name
to something red

Summer Away

I threaten to remember none of it. Hair cleansed of salt, Shi shrugs off her pain into the prairie wind. I imagine her dipped to the neck in a nighttime lake. A painless reason to miss my call. Ada calls me back before I call her, leg pinned under a log, signed by names I wouldn't recognize. The factory in her hometown sends me a keychain, a little can of salmon, and I lose it. I worry about how the sludge might soften her brain, slurry her words. Look, we've all been somewhere. I threaten to not know how to return. I threaten it all when the ambulance picks me up in the alley. Stomach pumped of colour and filled with black, I break free. Back to the back of the line again. Better to stay put, so they can come find me.

Dinner Party

Did you hear about the time
an ape chased us through the jungle?
We don't tell that story anymore.
We used to tell it often.

We don't tell it anymore.
3 oz of wine at dinnertime.
We got a dog, a job, a blog.
I fell backwards as he climbed.

Dinner parties end at 8.
I watch the headlights from the garden.
He was this close and this big.
I think about him often.

You lean back in your chair.
I tuck a hair into my bun.
You had a rock, I had a stick.
We weren't supposed to run.

I need no help in the kitchen.
Dog smiles in his sleep.
You were neon from the river.
I could smell his rotting teeth.

If only we'd lost our faces.
Gotten closer.
Risked a photo.
Held our places.

An ape chased us through the jungle.
Mmhm yes, it is getting colder.
You know how the ending goes.
We survived, got older.

Walking the Dog

He takes me to the park
to show me the world again,

what's green and brown
and red all over.

A neighbour says
show me your teeth

and we both give him a grin,
a neighbour we lived above

yet barely knew.
No longer a weapon,

we reclaim the stick.
He throws it for himself,

a joyful fling. He doesn't need me,
a tall, bald anomaly, but I need him.

I need him and Mark, downstairs.
The brownstone beside us, their cartwheels

and piano lessons. The widow across
who laughs when she walks.

To be less lost. Missed when we go.
Ricky and Max in the house down the road.

His wife nearly died. Max grew two sizes
in the years that we've known them.

The mailman, the butcher,
the coffee shop coders,

they all crowd for him:
belly up, taking submissions.

He reminds me to ask
and remember their names.

He does the same,
pushes his head into their shins.

I do it for him. I lift him up stairs.
Hand into jaws. Knees on the grass.

I'm here again, where I was at birth.
He wants to show me what he found in the dirt.

Parakeet at the Dog Park

Spot the neon parakeet that blooms
alongside the chickadees, blooms up
from the field as the young dog runs
through them, as the owner chases
the dog only to kiss him on the nose,
and he was a good boy, he acted out
his true nature, and the parakeet
was a good boy too, in that
he's been making the best
of a tough situation, so far
from his caged comforts,
chewing worms, and if I'm
to be a good boy I just need
to shower every two days,
make the bed, give and receive
pleasure and write a poem,
or should I run
through it like the dog,
or should I just run —

Bathroom Code

It unlocked everything.

We tried it on all the bikes, padlocks,

and cellphones in the city. Click. Click.

On and on we went, our bounty baubling.

We broke into a yacht and set sail,

your beautiful hair a shock around you.

I held my body back to mimic your shape.

The boat eventually sank, the bikes rusted

and I don't have your number anymore.

And when you cry out of your window —

I'd know it anywhere, it's a fawn

slipping into the mud, it's cloth ripping

— when you cry out the unlocked window,

I don't pretend to hear it at all.

Five Star Review for Bath Towel

IT WAS BEAUTIFUL.
Pulling at the thread
you'd unpicked
until a ladder grew,
close enough to heaven.
Of all that we've shared,
it's the only concrete:
holding what remains of
the river to your ankle bone,
my curl's outpourings,
whatever else we couldn't drink.
It was beautiful
and big enough.

Morning After and After That

You woke up on the mattress in the hallway.
We wrote something bad and threw it away.

Your old car died running up that hill.
We made the deal: friends until —

You left for years and then came back.
My throat bare for you, tongue left slacked.

I remember: you pulled me out by the ankles.
I was sick of your love so I never thanked you.

I was crawling for you, then I went quiet.
Your finger hooked in my cheek as we're driving.

And you loved me then, in spite of my errors.
I drank through your currency, slept on your caring.

Then let this be my final token.
A kinder mirror. A rhyming poem.

Swan Song

It's a myth that swans sing only once, right before they die.
In fact, they're as angry and silent as ever as they float
off into their celestial hole. I barrel towards death
with delightful regret. It's impossible to live every possible life.
All we can do is throw what's yet to be done —
the stolen kiss, the parachute, the unborn —
into the bag of holding with our spoils,
our spouses, the soy wax dried to the bath mat,
and hope to forget which was which.
I am happy to have seen the leaves turn again,
and to watch you pull a comb through your black hair.
To sing about it would be false. To write it down is just enough.

Acknowledgements

Gratitude to the editors at *Maisonneuve*, *Literary Review of Canada*, *PRISM International*, *CV2*, *This Magazine*, *TIFA* and *The Malahat Review*, who published or recognized some of these poems.

Further gratitude to Palimpsest Press, especially Aimee Dunn and Jim Johnstone — so happy to have the band back together for round two. Ellie Hastings — for the brilliant layout and design. And to Suzannah Showler and Sarah Venart, for your kind faith in these poems.

To the writers and best friends who joined me at these tables, on this endless night — every word is in celebration of you. I hope I got some of it right.

To my parents and my sister — I love you! We made it! Thank you for the rides and the nachos.

To Vincent, for seeing me home, and to our daughter Zoë, for completing it.

Photo Credit: Grady Mitchell

Michelle Brown's first book of poetry, *Safe Words* (Palimpsest Press), was a finalist for the 2018 ReLit Awards. She's had poems appear in *The Walrus*, *Maisonneuve*, *Literary Review of Canada*, *This Magazine* and *CV2*, amongst others. After nearly a decade in Toronto, she recently returned to the West Coast and now resides in Vancouver, BC.